You Want Me to Do *What?*

A Short Chronical
of a Long Teaching Life

by
CAROL HARRIS

ISBN: 1986390225
ISBN-13: 978-1986390224

DEDICATION

To my real family and my family of friends.

And especially Ron.

CONTENTS

Chapter 1
BEFORE THE BELL RINGS

Look, Look. Look and See.

See Carol in first grade learning to read from the big book placed on a round table for all the students to see.

I always wanted to be a teacher. No, that's not exactly true. At first I wanted to be a shoe sales person for then I would be able to go into that mysterious place behind the curtained doorway where all the shoe boxes were kept. As a first grade student, each day after school I would walk home and then start school all over again. I placed my dolls and stuffed animals around my playroom to be my silent students. Then I would reprimand them for all their misdeeds, just as my first grade teacher had done in my class. That was my overall impression of first grade: hollering at kids.

I taught a family friend's son how to swim after I became a really good swimmer and a lifeguard. That was my first teaching job. No hollering involved. It seemed like the most natural thing to be able to do; to break down

1

the essential elements of swimming and then put them together so he could learn. I now realize that I must have had some good instructors myself. I also had the good fortune to have had some stumbling blocks to overcome as a student. Not everything came easily to me, so I used my own difficulties as inspiration to be a better teacher when I had students who struggled.

I was a music education major in college. I spent my first two years teaching classroom music. However the majority of my thirty-three years of public school teaching was in general education classrooms, grades K through 5, in Southern California. I took time off from teaching when my two children were born, and didn't return to teaching until the younger one entered first grade. During that hiatus I earned a second teaching credential for grades K-9, taking one class per semester.

Patience, humor, love, joy, excitement, music and creativity were the tools I used in my teaching that were not found in the curriculum guides, and were not taught in my teacher preparation classes. I discovered these tools through my students, their parents, my colleagues, and mostly from the situations that arose each day. Watching my students acquire new skills made for meaningful and fulfilling years as a teacher.

When a person decides on a teaching career, for whatever reasons, she is given training in how to teach the subject matter, but there is more to teaching than that. I taught the assigned curriculum and was a very successful teacher in that regard. It was gratifying to witness the growth of my students but following a curriculum guide is merely the beginning of the teaching process. I found that choosing how to deliver this material was satisfying and creative. For it is essential to know the strengths, weaknesses, and interests of your students, and then tailor your lessons accordingly. It takes time to learn about each class, and to create an environment that fosters learning, cooperation, and a sense of inclusion for each student.

I have great memories of the many incredibly bright, sweet, quirky, funny, enjoyable, lively, sad, kind, brave, strong, and talented students that it has been my pleasure to have taught. As a bonus, my husband, a musician, was happy to share his musical talents with many of my classes, so my teaching became something integral to both of us.

I am still in contact with some of my former students and their families. Perhaps this book will open up the possibility of hearing from more of them. As precious as these people were and still are to me, that is not what this book is about. Perhaps the title may be a clue.

Teachers must be experts in curriculum and its delivery, classroom behavior management, and setting the tone in the classroom. Additionally, a teacher is expected to be responsible for attendance records, responding quickly to parent inquiries, attending all sorts of meetings, keeping the room clean, and, in the case of kindergarten, keeping zippers zipped, shoelaces tied, toilets flushed, keeping poop off the floor, hands washed, lunches and snacks ant-free, kids safely returned to their proper care-giver at the end of the day, with noses wiped. All while keeping a sharp eye out for head lice. Multi-tasking on such a large scale can only be understood by facing it person.

It was amazing to me that some student teachers came to teach in my classroom at the end of their college preparation, having never observed or helped in an elementary classroom. How could they possibly invest all that time, energy and money towards an unknown career? Teaching is not for everyone. New teachers need to complete an undergraduate degree, another year of curriculum and teacher prep classes, student teaching, probably three high stakes tests and at least three preparatory courses in how to teach students for whom English is not their primary language. They must also take at least one special training course in how to deal with students with special needs, since there is limited support for them once they are in your classroom. Additionally, some become teachers without having a supervising teacher or student teaching experience. They learn the ropes with another novice and make their way by the seat of their pants. I don't believe this is the optimal method for training a teacher. There surely exists statistics on how long new teachers remain in the profession, and if this correlates to their initial training.

If you are reading this book because you have decided to become a teacher, I hope this short memoir will answer the questions that educators don't ask, no less answer. Some of these stories may remind you of your own experiences as a young student. If you are a parent, you might find a better understanding of the kinds of situations that can come up in school. If you are already a teacher, be prepared to smile or cringe in recognition.

Teachers can expect to be privy to comical, heart-wrenching and profound moments that will help shape your ability to respond with reason and compassion, incrementally adding to your own life's lessons, changed for the better by your work.

There is one more very big thing that no one, except a very thorough master teacher, is likely to warn you about: you will have a great many unreasonable requests made of you. Once you begin teaching, something will be asked of you that is not found in any curriculum guide, something way beyond what your contract even hints at as being your responsibility. However you respond to this request, you might really wish you could exclaim, "You want me to do what?" I never used these words but I came close. Instead, I wrote the requests down for future telling. Perhaps you'll be inclined to do the same.

In the stories that follow, whenever there is a mention of student names, I will not use a child's real name. If you happen to find yourself in this book, I thank you for your contribution. I am grateful to all my students and their parents for having made my life richer.

The first story I will tell you is the one that prompted me to write this book.

Chapter 2
PARENT REQUESTS

You Want Me to Do WHAT?

Sometimes my husband and I were invited to dinner at the homes of my students and their families. These were generally very special and sweet occasions for us both. One of these dinners was especially memorable.

On this particular evening, we were at the home of my student, Beverly. Her older sister, Karen, had also been my student. Beverly's family also included a younger sister, a father, and a mother who also happened to be our family's veterinarian.

Beverly had been planning for this evening for a month. She had carefully selected the menu which included meatloaf, her favorite, and many other delicious dishes. It was a lively dinner: there were no shy people in this family. After eating, Beverly wanted to show me her room, upstairs. I went there with the three girls and their mom, and I was treated to the full, three-excited-girls tour. It included the hallway, where Beverly showed me she had set up a tea-party table, chairs, plates, cups, and dolls, where she liked to play. She demonstrated how she played and showed me that she had some very special, highly polished, flat, smooth, rather large colored stones that she used as pretend food and drinks. Beverly placed one stone in her cup and lifted the cup to her lips. She sipped her *tea* but she accidentally swallowed the stone! Her eyes showed the horror of what she did, as did mine! She swallowed deeply, was able to breathe, and could speak, but was definitely shaken. I ran for her mom who was just inside the doorway and told her what happened.

Being a vet, she knew that a stone swallowed by an animal would result in a necessary surgery! I reminded her that, since we walk upright, I thought it might be okay, although perhaps uncomfortable for Beverly. But it was certainly something to check on with the doctor immediately, which she did.

I went downstairs and told Beverly's dad what had just happened. Moments later, in walked Beverly and her mom, both of them smiling. Mom was carrying two items. She explained that, indeed, I was correct. Beverly would be just fine and the stone would *pass* in a day or two. But it would be essential to make sure that it *did* make an exit. Therefore, I should take to school a roll of Saran Wrap and the rubber gloves she was holding out for me. For the next few days, whenever Beverly needed to go to the bathroom, I was to line the toilet seat with the plastic, and if she passed any stool, I was to check it. Using the gloves, of course!

I did some quick thinking. As my mind sped ahead to the next few days, these are the things I discussed with Beverly's parents: I would have had a class of thirty two cherubs waiting in the classroom alone if I went into the adjoining bathroom with Beverly, as well as being *alone* in a bathroom with Beverly. How many things were wrong with this picture? Absolutely everything. And that didn't include the inspection of the saran wrap!

The visit ended rather quickly following this

misadventure. We had already shared a wonderful dessert and great excitement so the evening was complete.

If this had been most any other family, I probably would have told the mom that it would be best to keep Beverly home until the stone had *left the building*, so to speak. However, this was no ordinary relationship, so I determined that the next day I would enlist the help of our health clerk, whose office was just next door to my classroom.

Mine was the first request she had ever had like this, and she laughed, but was agreeable. After a couple of days of going to the health office whenever she needed to use the bathroom, Beverly had had no positive results.

On the third day after school, I received a phone call in my classroom. Beverly was on the line. She had gone out to lunch for sushi with her mom, and had used the bathroom at the restaurant. Beverly had exciting news for me. The stone had come out! I was very relieved and happy for her, and we talked about her adventure. Then she got quiet, and paused, and then told me the sad part of her story. She was not keeping the rock, even though it was her favorite rock.

When Beverly graduated from high school, I sent her a congratulatory letter and, of course, a stone.

* * *

I had been a voice major in college, so it was natural for me to sing a great deal with my classes. I used an autoharp for accompaniment. One afternoon, following dismissal, Eileen's dad asked if he could speak with me. Our conversation went something like this:

"Mrs. Harris, you sing such wonderful songs with your class. I hear Eileen singing them at home every day."

"I'm so glad she sings them for you."

"It would be great to have them in a songbook, because I'm not familiar with some of the songs that she sings. Have you ever considered writing them all down in a Mrs. Harris songbook?"

"I know what you mean. Sometimes it's hard to know exactly what it is kids are singing when they sing the songs alone. I'm so glad Eileen loves to sing so much! No, I've never put together a song book. First of all, they are not my songs, so it wouldn't exactly be right to print out all the words."

"Oh, I would need more than just the words," he said. "It's kind of hard to tell what tune Eileen is actually singing, so I'd need to see the melody as well."

"Really? You want me to write out all the music with the words, too?"

"Right, and also the chords so I can play them on my guitar."

"Oh, my" (or something to that effect). Probably many of them are not even written down anywhere. I've just learned them and remembered them over the years. (This conversation took place long before the Internet was available.) Do you realize what a huge request you are making?"

"And (without pausing to acknowledge what I just said) could you show me *how* to play the chords on the guitar, too?"

"You want me to do what?" Did I play guitar? No.

*   *   *

Kerry was a small, thin, pale boy with great big problems of control. Knowing this before school began, I visited him at his house to help establish a personal connection with him. The previous spring his mother had come to school for a meeting, which I attended. She told us then that Kerry had been "kicked out" of numerous nursery schools. She and her husband were very busy people and really didn't know what to do with him. Kerry was indeed a handful, not only for me but for my students, as well. On the play yard he would crouch down low in the bushes when the bell rang for recess to be over. Luckily we had extremely low bushes and he wore brightly colored shirts so I could always see him. He admired Sammy, another student in the class, who was much more physically skilled than Kerry. Kerry desperately wanted attention from Sammy. He tried many ways and finally achieved contact. He threw a really large rock and hit Sammy's head, causing bruising and a large lump. After taking Sammy to the nurse, I took the rock and Kerry to my principal. She called Kerry's parents and told them about the incident. She kept the rock on her desk for the rest of the year. We thought that Kerry's parents would make a concerned call to Sammy's parents, at least to find out how he was. This never happened. A couple of weeks passed. Kerry's mom came to school and showed me a certificate from a karate studio where Kerry was now a student. His Mom requested that when I spoke Kerry's name he was, in the style of respect he learned in karate practice, to drop to one knee and address me in a certain manner. At that point I would know that I had his attention and he would then say, "Yes, Mrs. Harris." This was all written out in a letter to me.

Without missing a beat I told Kerry's mom that this was not going to happen in my class. I still have that unique letter tucked away.

*   *   *

I have received many lovely gifts from the students whom I have taught. Along with the gifts, I have enjoyed the heartfelt cards and letters expressing gratitude for my kindness, patience and even my sense of humor. I especially appreciated the student-made notes.

I ask myself why it is that I also remember the parent who could never express gratitude. Could it be that it was because I was tested daily by her child, and by her? Was it because she unsuccessfully tried to have her daughter transferred from my class when I had back surgery and had to be out of the class for several weeks? I had a magnificent substitute teacher in my room and we were in daily contact. No. It had to do with a simple story of lost and found, and common courtesy. And it went like this:

Shortly after dismissal from kindergarten one day, Karen and her mom returned to the classroom. Mrs. K explained that she was so excited to see Karen after school that she gave her an exceptionally big hug and in the process lost a precious earring. I asked her where she was when this enormous hug took place and I started to help her look for it. We were just outside the classroom door. In reality I was the only one doing any looking. Mrs. K proceeded to tell me how valuable this earring was, not only monetarily, but sentimentally to her. It had belonged to her grandmother, it was an antique setting, it was irreplaceable, it meant a great deal to her...while I continued, *alone*, to search the ground. I asked her if she had looked in her car, on her path to it, and around the car doors. I retrieved a flashlight from the classroom emergency bag to help in the search. Still, *I* was doing the searching while listening to Mrs. K's patter. I felt like Cinderella. After quite a while of looking, bending and sifting through bits of scattered litter, I was ready to give up, when my flashlight passed over the door jam and I noticed something sparkle in the crack. Sure enough, it was the prized diamond earring. I stooped down, once again, retrieved it, and asked,

"Could this be it?"

Mrs. K squealed, snatched it up, took her daughter and away they went.

I considered that half-hour or so a success. The rest of the day was uneventful. The following day Karen mentioned to me that her mom was really happy that she had her earring back. *That* must have been my thank you.

It has been many years since that lost and found event, yet I can still recall the feelings I was left with from this encounter. Mrs. K's lack of courtesy simply confirmed the negative feelings I had towards her on so many levels. I wonder what my hourly rate *should* have been for my search. This activity certainly was not included in the teacher contract.

Acts of simple courtesy cost very little and come in many forms. Eye contact and a smile can work wonders. So do words of thanks. A short note, an email or a phone call are all appreciated. Do you remember, as a young child, your Mom reminding you to say thank you to other people? I never liked it, as everyone could always hear that reminder being given. I groaned internally every time I had to remind my own children as they were learning this important life skill. As an adult, the lack of this skill is unfortunate. It also speaks volumes about the person who does not acknowledge something helpful.

Lately I've become aware that when I say, "Thank you," a typical response is,

"No problem."

I've discussed this phenomenon with my husband and my friends. It is a cause for jokes about how, when thanking a person for doing his job, his response is, "No problem."

I am sorely tempted to reply, "I wasn't expecting it to be a problem!"

Just now, as I was writing this chapter in the ER waiting room with my husband and his ailing gall bladder, a patient made an inquiry at the check-in desk, and obviously said,

"Thank you."

Loud and clear came the response, "No problem."

If Karen's Mom had thanked me, even a tiny bit for

finding her earring, I'm sure I would have responded with something more gracious than, "No problem."

*   *   *

One autumn day, I heard a child crying in the adjoining bathroom. My class had just gone outside for recess. We had two bathrooms in the room, and this one was obviously occupied. I knocked on the door and a very upset boy tried to talk to me through his tears. I asked if I could open the door just a bit to be able to understand him better. He agreed.

Ben had had a major case of diarrhea and both he and the bathroom needed a scouring! I reassured him and told him I would call his mother immediately. I made sure he had toilet paper - mostly to dry his eyes. Luckily, Ben's mom was home. While we waited for her to arrive, I kept close tabs on Ben but there was really nothing to be done by me to clean him up. His mom arrived with clean clothes. She was upset that I hadn't physically helped Ben. I explained that I really wasn't allowed to be alone with a student in the bathroom. She finally understood and was grateful that I had rounded up some clean water and lots of toilet paper for her to use. This was before Wet Wipes were invented. She thanked me profusely the next day.

Later in the spring, on a sizzling day of 103 degrees, with our classroom air conditioner on the fritz, Ben came up to where I was seated on a small chair in front of the class. He got these words out, "Mrs. Harris I," when what was really on his mind became apparent as he threw up all over me, from my head to the skirt of my dress. I had several things to worry about. The class voiced a variety of reactions – disgust, fear, and loud crying that matched Ben's. Believe me, I not only wanted to cry, but was trying to not throw up myself, my usual reaction to that easily identified odor. It was very hot in the room and Ben's vomit was now soaking not only the carpet, but through my clothing to my skin, including my scalp and face. Once again we were able to reach Ben's mom and she rescued Ben and thanked me. I wondered if this was our lucky karma with each other.

The only problem for me was that *my* Mommy couldn't come and rescue *me*. No one was available (or willing) to take over my class so I could go home and change. I was able to clean up my hair and face. But my clothes were stuck tightly to me, and oh, the smell! The heat seemed to warm it up and bake it to me. Everyone in room 2B was ready to go home a bit early that day!

Ben's mom thanked me again in a lovely note. And I hadn't even looked for a diamond earring for her. I knew she was sincere. And, after all, I *was* washable.

Chapter 3
PARENT CONFERENCES

Can We Talk?

Parent conferences are sometimes very beneficial, sometimes frustrating and, sometimes even fun and full of good humor. Depending on the circumstances and what is discussed, conferences can also be dramatic. Conference-training workshops that I took provided me with some helpful tools. One technique that I still remember and use to this day works in non-school situations as well. If you need a way to draw a discussion to a close when it seems it will never end, keep a pen at the ready – one with a removable cover. When you want to conclude a conference with someone who does not seem ready to leave, rise from your seated position and, using the pen cover, close the pen in an obvious way. It has the effect of announcing that this talk is over.

It is usually best to conference with all the parents of a child at the same time. This is especially true with divorced parents. I say "all," because, with marriage and remarriage, there can be many adults involved in a child's life. By having everyone present, the same information can be shared with all concerned, and there will be less chance that the conference will be misrepresented in a re-telling.

Some parents worry that kindergarten will be a needless lost year for their child who is already reading and computing. Parents of a particularly bright child will sometimes insist that their child be moved ahead to the next grade so he won't be bored. This is often a mistake from my perspective, as most children in that situation don't get bored at all. In any grade, if a classroom is structured in a way that allows children to create, read, write and formulate at their own levels of accomplishment, boredom is not a problem. There may be good reasons to move a child ahead, but boredom isn't one of them.

*   *   *

Neil was mature in his thinking. He was a very accomplished reader/writer in my kindergarten, already having developed these skills before school began. He was well-suited to being in kindergarten. He still benefitted from learning more about math and he needed more experience interacting with more aggressive, rough and tumble kids. Neil had a wonderful calm about him and my other students appreciated his kindnesses. One very outspoken boy raised his hand and felt compelled to share how much he admired Neil and how smart he was. A beautiful gesture from an opinionated classmate.

At my first conference with Neil's mother, she had only one question: "Would a computer at home help Neil?" She fooled me and I burst out laughing. I had been prepared for the usual grade-change request. She asked this sincere question at a time before home computers were standard stock in homes. Neil loved to write stories. His handwriting was well- developed. Improving his computer skills at home would be a plus and would be fun, too. So I said, "Sure." I explained my laughter and agreed that this could be a wonderful tool for Neil. Whenever we practiced basic skills in class that he had already mastered, Neil either read a book, wrote more stories, or just enjoyed practicing with the other students. He was never bored just because he was more advanced in some areas than others.

*   *   *

One year I had a question about a student of mine. I noticed one hot day when Forrest was wearing shorts to school, that his legs were a different size from one another. His mother had never mentioned anything about it to me. The next day when she dropped Forrest off, I asked her if she had some time after school for a short conference. From that moment until we actually met was three hours and twenty minutes of torture for this lovely lady! I had *not* done a good job of putting her mind at ease. His mom was on pins and needles until class was over and we could talk. I felt badly that she had suffered so. After that, whenever I made a conference request I was careful not to alarm the parents unnecessarily.

Her child, Forrest, an absolutely brilliant boy, came up with one of my all-time favorite quotes about the state of practicing things in kindergarten. It was a difficult task for him to form the letters of the alphabet using a pencil. In those days we had our students choose one center each day that they would work at, eventually getting to each of the five centers during the week. Forrest always put off the writing center for last, hoping that Friday would just fall off the earth, I suppose. I recognized his strategy, so one day I asked him why he did this. Forrest had a highly developed vocabulary and was also bilingual. He explained his reason quite colorfully to me, "This center makes me constipated."

I didn't laugh, but I totally understood. In all probability it *did* make him constipated, even though the word he probably meant to use was *frustrated.* His little hand and finger muscles were just not ready for the task of writing, but I was making him try it. He knew he was not doing a perfect job - thus, the constipation. Forrest did learn how to write very well in his own time. I later learned that he went on to do extremely well in school, followed by a wonderful career. And his penmanship was excellent.

Sometimes parents think it is fine to start an a*d hoc* conference with you as they drop off or pick up their child. It's a mistake that arises from a parent's understandable focus on her own child. It is also an easy conversation starter with her child's teacher. Any parent teacher conference is too important to receive divided attention from the teacher and a public conference is just wrong.

*   *   *

There are a number of memories that make me cringe at what I did or said to parents, but one particular encounter stands out in my mind. I had a kindergarten student, Felicia, whose parents had emigrated from China. She was a very bright girl who was not interacting with any other children in the class. Her English skills were good, but her social skills needed help. During my conference with her father I explained that Felicia was doing very well academically but that there was another aspect of school that she needed help with. He was very interested in assisting at home. I offered to lend him a few books of mine that might be helpful, and we continued talking as I kneeled down on the floor, digging through the back of a deep cabinet where my personal books were stashed. I asked if he and his wife had ever read any books on child-rearing in China. There was a very long silence in the room. I looked up from my digging to see him shaking his head with an unusual expression on his face. He then quietly replied, "You see, they burned all our books."

I apologized for my mistake. I had erroneously thought that, as with all the other Chinese families I had come in contact with, his family came from Hong Kong, not mainland China. Loaning him my books, I made sure he had a public library card so he could find more books on this subject. He was very kind in spite of my false assumption.

Felicia graduated from high school recently and is now attending UC Berkeley. No doubt she made use of many libraries, computer terminals and books. I received the loveliest letter from her family at the end of kindergarten which I now have framed and hanging on my wall at home. It includes this Chinese saying: *being a teacher for one day means being a father/mother for a whole life.*

*   *   *

One unusual conference I had involved two divorced parents. They had not really talked together for a while and used our conference as an opportunity to catch up on their many relatives on both sides...new births, important events, and how Aunt Mary was doing since her surgery. It was lovely to see this couple getting along so well, but I had great difficulty breaking into their reunion party to try to give them information about their son, Daniel! I would interject by saying, "You might be interested in how well his small motor skills are developing," and "Getting back to Daniel...." It was my first and only such conference. I felt as though I should have been serving tea and cookies for them. Who knows, maybe something blossomed during that conference!

*   *   *

Then there was the conference with a mom about her daughter, Lydia. The mom was so angry at her husband, that she wasn't interested in hearing about Lydia, her youngest child in a large family. She let me know that she had been through many parent-teacher conferences and had "heard it all many times before." She kept bringing our conference around to the fact that she wasn't having sex with her husband. No, she was not asking me for advice. Yes, she was very skilled at avoiding hearing about Lydia. Apparently, she confused the parent-teacher conference with a session with a therapist. I was dumbfounded, to say the least. I was barely able to have her sign the report card and leave so I could meet with the next parent who was waiting outside the room.

*   *   *

I was puzzled when Tony's father came to our conference wearing sunglasses, indoors, and wore them the whole time we spoke about his son. I kept wondering why, but, due to his other somewhat strange mannerisms, I was too intimidated to ask. Was he hiding red eyes? Did he want to remain incognito? Did he forget his regular glasses? Perhaps he accomplished his goal of finding out how long it would take me to ask? I didn't ask. There were many more important issues to discuss. I recently saw the father's name on the door in a medical building. He is an osteopath. Perhaps I should make an appointment so I can finally ask about the glasses.

*   *   *

My most frightening conference occurred when an enraged father stormed into my classroom, just as school was beginning. He wanted to know if I was Mrs. Harris, and then thunderously demanded that we talk right then. I had no idea who he was, and asked him who his child was. I told him that I couldn't speak with him then, since school had started. He got his face right up close to mine and screamed at me, "You'll talk to me when I say you will!" I was scared that he was going to pull a knife or a gun and kill me...and in front of my students!

Fortunately, another student's mom was in the room. I turned to her and asked her to watch my class. I then asked Mr. L if he was going to leave the room. He declined. I told him that if he wasn't going to leave the room, then I would. I turned quickly and went out the door. I could feel that he was hot on my heels. I had no idea what I was going to do, but I knew that I needed him to leave the room full of children! I went into the class that was in session next door, pulled open the door and interrupted the teacher. Mr. L followed me into the room. I blurted out, "Miss Weaver, can you watch my class for me? Mr. L won't leave the classroom and I can't have him in there!"

The astonished look on my poor teammate's face bordered on comedy mixed with confusion. I suppose that I made my point to Mr. L that we were *not* about to talk then. My teammate agreed to help. Mr. L huffed away, muttering something to the effect that he would be back. That's when my body started shaking and the tears flowed. It took a long time to compose myself even after I went back to my room. That lovely mom stayed in class for a while, just to support me. I told my students that I was very upset, as though they couldn't tell, but that we were going to proceed with the regular morning business, as usual. Before she left, the witnessing mom told me that she would be happy to corroborate what had happened. Bless her!

In those days, at that school there was no way to communicate with the school office from the classrooms. Following this drama and the conference I insisted on having with the principal and both Mr. and Mrs. L later that week, the school installed a phone system, because for that entire scary morning, until my break, I had no way to call for help if Mr. L returned. Until lunch time I kept the door locked and watched out the windows for him to return. He didn't. I was very thankful.

Many more events related to this student happened throughout the year, but by then his father was banned from the campus without an appointment. In light of the many shootings that are now occurring in our country, as I revisit this enraged conference request, I feel that full terror wash over me again. What good would a *ban* do if he really had mayhem on his agenda? Following our evening conference, I was fearful for the safety of my own children, even though I did not live near the school. My husband was on a business trip and I felt very vulnerable.

*   *   *

Evy's father came to her first kindergarten conference. His wife was unable to attend. He seemed apprehensive until I showed him some of Evy's work and told him what a lovely girl she was. At one point in our conversation he started to cry. I was startled and asked him why, as I passed him the box of tissues. It turned out that he was very nervous about Evy, his second daughter, and was incredibly relieved by the positive things I was saying and showing him. Evy was a very empathetic girl and loved to help out with both her peers and any adults who needed help or a friendly smile. She told me that I wouldn't have to send home any letters about homework, as her mother was a psychic and would already know the assignment. One day, on a field trip to a facility that trained seeing eye dogs, a woman from the center was speaking with my class about what they would be observing. Karen, a little girl who had major difficulties in speaking, raised her hand. The woman called on

Karen, and then waited. And waited. And then asked Karen what she wanted to say. Karen was stumbling in getting her speech out. Before I could jump in to explain, Evy took care of everything by saying, "It just takes her longer to say her words." I'm not sure if I had ever actually explained this to the class, as Karen was always raising her hand. On her own, Evy had learned the important lesson of patience and understanding well beyond her five years of age.

*   *   *

Most parents are pleased to hear about the progress their child is making. Even if the steps are small, they are necessary, and they certainly are cumulative. More importantly, they add to a child's confidence about himself as a capable learner. I felt privileged to be able to observe some of these moments of progress and share them with parents.

Brandon had a very difficult time writing the capital letter R. His hand just wouldn't cooperate with his brain, no matter how much he tried. He tried hard for days, becoming frustrated with his efforts. I encouraged him and assured him that he would soon get it. I suggested that he take a break in his struggles but he was tenacious. Brandon had this *do it 'til I get it* attitude. His excitement was delicious on the day that he discovered all his practice had finally paid off and he was now an expert R writer. He went around the room celebrating by writing all the words he could find that had an R in them.

I was happy to report this to his parents that evening, and they were thrilled. To this day, Brandon approaches all tasks that he wants to achieve in just this same, focused manner. It was nothing that I taught him, just his own personal approach to learning. Brandon became a prolific writer. He is now attending Brown University...no doubt writing without the aid of pencil or pen, and using many words that have an R in them.

It's gratifying to observe parents who support their children in all the small steps they take that eventually add up to the whole. It's also gratifying to watch as a child realizes true achievement in small tasks which is a reward in and of itself. No candy or other bribes needed. Unfortunately there are many ways to negatively affect a child's opinion of himself as a capable learner.

*   *   *

When I taught fifth grade for a year I found it difficult to grade those students who worked "below grade level" but were working very hard. My principal explained that I could use asterisks and give a grade of B* with an explanation. I was very relieved and did this happily. So it was disheartening when one student, Kyle, returned his report card with his mother's signature and comment of, "Why didn't you just give him an F?" Kyle had a younger brother for whom school was a snap. Kyle was a dedicated student who just came to learning some things a little slower, and certainly didn't deserve this harsh sentence in my mind.

Now, 45 years later, I still use a set of ceramic bowls his family gave me as a gift. I think of Kyle each time I use them, and wonder how he is doing. I hope he learned that there is so much more in life than grades, or being compared to your brother. But school lasts a long time and many lessons that are not in text books are learned there, both positive and negative.

*   *   *

In the same vein...

Many years later, in kindergarten, Cory wasn't sure about how to identify a specific letter of the alphabet while working with me. He asked for help and in good teacher form, I asked him back how he could figure it out. He looked around the room until he found the alphabet chart on the wall. Then he recited the alphabet, pointing to each letter until he came to the one he wanted. He checked with me that it was the right one, and it was. I was very proud of how he knew to use the resources in the room to find out what he needed, and so was he. Yet when I reported this breakthrough to his mom, she really didn't want to hear this as good news, more as a deficiency of his, to not already know his letters. She also unfavorably compared him to his younger brother.

That school year passed and Cory was now in first grade. His mom, Mrs. P, came to my classroom after school hours, to complain about Cory's first grade teacher. I told her I had never seen this person teach and that the principal was really the person she should speak to. Mrs. P ignored this information and resumed her litany of reasons for why this teacher was not any good. We stood the whole time that we spoke because I was standing when she burst in on me. I was not going to make this forceful intrusion into my personal time a friendly, comfortable chat, so we did not sit down. My teammate from the room next door could see what was going on through our common window. From time to time she would make some funny eyebrow expressions and hand motions to me that I could not return. Unfortunately we had never prepared a signal that would mean *come and rescue me from this difficult situation!*

After forty minutes I could tell there was no easy way to get rid of this complaining parent. I repeated that I could do nothing about her concerns, and reiterated that she should really speak to the teacher or the principal. I repeated that she had anger that I couldn't help her with and that I didn't understand why she had come to tell me. I also realized that there was nothing, absolutely nothing that I was doing that would get her *out* of my room and make her stop harassing me. A cap on the pen would accomplish nothing in this case. And I wanted her out!

In hindsight, if I had had the presence of mind to think clearly after her extended visit, I should have walked her to the school office, again pointing out that she should share her concerns with the principal. If the principal was not available, I should have arranged an appointment. But I was not thinking clearly.

I remember what I said next because I wrote it down at the time. I said exactly this: "Mrs. P, you have to remember, this is public education. And if you don't like it, there's the door." As I spoke these words, I pointed to the front classroom door. It worked like a charm. She left through that door without another word. And she never spoke to me again.

This was fine with me. And really, I only spoke the truth. I don't know if she ever went to the principal or not. She had just wanted to complain. I was really the wrong person to talk to. All I wanted to do was finish my work that was keeping me at school long after my official work time was over.

Several years later, I mentioned this incident to my principal. She was *horrified* to learn what I told the mom. I related the fact that I found no other way to end the conversation, and that really, I said nothing untrue. She admitted as much, but was still shocked. When I reflect on the event, I am a bit shocked, too, but I *really* was at my wit's end. I'm still unsure why Mrs. P came to me in the first place. Was it a *get even* move on her part to begin with, showing me how dissatisfied she had been with me as well? I'll never know.

* * *

Back to School Night for parents is an opportunity for teachers to share their plans for the coming year as well as a chance for parents to get a feeling about the teacher who will be influencing their child for the next ten months. It can relieve or cause a lot of stress.

I had been teaching at a school for three years already and felt secure about parents trusting my abilities. This particular year I wanted to explain to parents that my mind might be a bit distracted: my daughter was being married in October, so if they had a request, it would be best to put it in writing, rather than trusting it to my memory. Again, this was in the years before computers, email or smart phones.

As I was explaining about the wedding, I became a bit emotional when I said, "My daughter is being married in two weeks." My inner ear heard it as the voice of Mary Tyler Moore when she would sort of warble, "Mr. Grant..." Parents chuckled and I got on with the business of the evening.

Several weeks later Mona, a girl in this class, had been absent for a couple of days. Her older sister came to my room to pick up any work I could give her for Mona to do at home. She gave me a message which was, "My mother says to tell you she is sorry about your daughter." I didn't understand, so I asked her to repeat what she said. I'm really quite good about asking people to repeat themselves. I then asked her why her mother was sorry. Her mother, it turned out, was sorry my daughter had died. I still didn't understand, but I knew there was some reason for this. The mother had been born in Vietnam but it seemed to me that her English was very good. I thanked the older daughter and told her not to worry, and to please tell her mother that my daughter had not died.

It was a mystery to me. I mentioned this to a colleague, describing what I had said at the evening meeting. She figured it out quickly. When I said "married" it probably came out more like I had a cold and was heard by this mom as "buried."

*　　　*　　　*

For several years my kindergarten teammates and I presented the Back to School Night basics together in the Multi-Purpose Room, and then finished up in our individual classrooms. During this combined assembly, in true kindergarten style, I sang the song, "Plant a Radish", while my teammates provided backup with visuals, just as we might present a lesson in class. The humorous lyrics of the song compared planting a known entity of vegetable seeds and their resulting harvests, as opposed to the *unknowns* of raising a child. We thought it was apropos. I would have liked to sing the Stephen Sondheim song, "Children Will Listen", on these occasions. Since I am not Bernadette Peters, I never had the courage. The words and sentiments of the song are very strong and wise in the ways that children learn. They impart a strong warning about unintended learning, learning based not just on our words but our actions as well. The song alone could have saved many minutes of presentation. Perhaps you will agree and be brave enough in a parent discussion to break out in song someday. It would be handy to have a piano accompanist on call.

Chapter 4
LEARNING FROM MY STUDENTS

In the introduction to the song from The King and I, "Getting to Know You," Oscar Hammerstein II had it right: ". . . by your pupils you'll be taught". A teacher is also a student. Always. When you are awarded a teaching credential it doesn't signify the completion of your education. Instead, it's just the beginning of a new and exciting phase of your learning. You become an autodidact. Self-educated.

Teachers come across situations that call upon their ability to evaluate, respond, and do what is right for all their students. Sensitivity training needs to be emphasized in teacher preparation classes. Since it's not, teachers learn on the job.

We have moments that call for the wisdom of Solomon. These moments can last mere seconds but the results of a teacher's response can make all the difference in the life of a child. I am especially grateful to my second grade teacher, Mrs. Cornelius, for her wisdom.

Every day after lunch, Mrs. Cornelius would have us sit at our desks, heads down if we wished, recovering from our active play. She would walk around the room, poetry book in hand, and recite poems. Over time, we were supposed to learn these poems by heart and recite them with her. Mrs. Cornelius would hold the small book in one hand, and use her other hand to indicate the flow of the words, the rise and fall of her voice, and any other dramatic emphasis she wanted us to learn. I loved these moments, although I had trouble learning the poems very quickly this way.

One day, without warning, Mrs. Cornelius asked me to take over leading this activity. I was a fluent reader and so had no problem with the words. In fact, now that I could *see* the words I could recite them much better. I was definitely a visual learner. I don't think that in the fifties this expression was used, but Mrs. Cornelius must have instinctively known what I needed. Not only did she teach me to walk and read, without tripping or bumping into obstacles, she showed me how to hold the book just as she did, in one hand, using the other hand to indicate expressiveness. This was my very first experience in choral conducting.

I can recall this scene well and I realize what a unique learning experience it had become. As I remember it, no one else ever had this honor, and I became the daily, afternoon poetry leader. I loved it! Perhaps this is one reason that when I became a teacher I had my own students learning and reciting poetry and why I love singing choral music so much. Thank you, Mrs. Cornelius.

Another vivid lesson, including how people learn, happened to me at a summer camp which met each day during the week. This time the credit didn't go to the teacher. I was the one who figured it out. A daily swim class was a cooling and refreshing relief from the heat of the summer. I was already a swimmer, but at this camp I was confounded by trying to learn the breast stroke. I was not able to move my arms and my legs to work in the rhythm of pulling and then pushing with a frog kick, while synchronizing my breathing with it all. The more I tried, the more frustrated I became, and the louder and more insistently the swim teacher yelled at me.

Let's begin with the word *louder*. There was nothing wrong with my hearing. So now, since she was yelling at me, everyone could hear about my difficulty. Embarrassment set in immediately, and my operating systems shut down. Now I wanted to vanish.

The instruction never changed. Obviously, I wasn't learning the mechanics of this stroke but I didn't have any alternatives to try. I don't remember any of the instructions that were screamed at me, but my overall feelings of failure and confusion remain with me to this day. Making it worse, in trying to learn, I was surrounded by successful swimmers as water seeped into my nose, mouth, and lungs.

This continued for a couple of days, until I refused to swim. Cajoling didn't break my resolve. I sat out and watched and listened, rehearsing the stroke and breathing and the rhythm of the whole stroke on dry land. No one paid attention to me, so the pressure was off.

The next day I hopped into the pool, and I had it! The breast stroke was mine. I don't know if the instructor learned anything from my experience, but I came away with the knowledge that being pressured and yelled at did not accomplish the goal of teaching me.

Translate this event into a classroom setting, and it's so clear to me that students need time to learn. Unpressured time. A chance to process learning. Try different approaches but above all, give it time. Some students *get it* immediately, some more gradually, and some need a chance to back off, and look at the skill from another perspective. But each student needs to have the pressure off and to be motivated to find a way to learn the task in his or her own way, and then enjoy the success.

What motivates each child to learn? It's not the same

for everyone. But think about a child, learning to walk. Even though she falls, sways, stumbles, maybe cries, and then gives up and crawls for a bit more, she always goes back to trying, practicing, and then becoming successful. Time and motivation are a powerful combination.

*   *   *

Through the years many students have come to my class without even knowing English. They have the incredible task of learning a new language as well as everything else they are expected to grasp. Put them in an environment where they feel as safe as can be arranged, where kids and the teacher are encouraging and positive, and they will learn faster and with confidence.

*   *   *

A young girl from China, Noelle, entered my kindergarten class, at the mid point of the school year without speaking any English. It so happened I was reading the Sandra Boynton book, *Oops,* to my class that day. It is a very silly, simple to understand, board picture book in which something funny happens on each page. Naturally, the class loved it. The humor released the nervousness Noelle had. Of course, her first English word was, "Oops." The rest of the class was into the silliness and fun of this word. It became our mantra for the rest of the year. Noelle taught me what a valuable tool humor is for dealing with nervousness.

*   *   *

Another student, another year, Nathan arrived two months before the end of school, having been adopted into his new family from a Russian orphanage. He had never been to school and he knew only a few words of English.

He was a loving child with an open, inquisitive mind, and an extremely strong determination to explore. The building blocks, the pencil sharpener, and the playhouse were all an exciting gift to Nathan. My class was very interested to learn that Nathan's beginnings in life had been so different than theirs. This naturally led to their need to know how Russian sounded, which gave Nathan a certain cool status in the room.

While my other students had already learned that they sometimes had to meet with me as a whole group for a lesson or activity, Nathan was oblivious to rules. At first I tried to encourage Nathan to join us, but he taught me that that wasn't always possible. He only joined us where the class met on the rug when I was reading a story or singing a song. When my other students questioned why Nathan could still play when they couldn't, I realized that Nathan reminded me what I really knew all along about young children: they need the freedom to explore and learn what they can about their environment, first and foremost. Only after they have satisfied that curiosity can they then focus on other, non self-initiated stimuli. This might explain why, after a teacher has talked for a long time, some students' minds drift on to something more interesting in their own heads. It should not always be explained as ADHD.

The following year, Nathan was again in my kindergarten class, ready to actually focus on what I was teaching. This time he was accustomed to the trappings of the classroom. As luck would have it, Nathan now had a fellow student, Mona, who was also Russian. They could speak to each other in Russian if they wanted to. By now, however, Nathan seemed to be rejecting most things Russian as he assimilated into his new American status, shedding a very difficult past life. He and Mona did become friends, even though she was a girl. She was a very accomplished and bright student. Little Nathan and tall Mona would sit together on the rug. It was a sweet friendship. And when Mona's grandmother would pick Mona up from school, she would always have a loving word for Nathan in Russian. He was extremely attentive the day Grandma shared some Russian Christmas customs and songs with the class.

I realize as I write about these two students, how literature was a constant in helping them learn the school culture. As for Nathan, he would snuggle, standing next to me when I read to the whole class. My students accepted this unique reading habit as okay. In fact, when the kids were reading their own small books, Nathan, in a similar way, preferred to sit close to one of his new friends, just as he had done with me.

*   *   *

These days we ask very young children to write sentences. They are supposed to spell the words correctly, and to use punctuation. We are told to expect youngsters to accomplish this even before some of them are capable of pronouncing words correctly. With encouragement and practice they will learn to approximate mature speech. While we, as adults, wait and provide practice and encouragement for them to achieve mature speech, some entertaining encounters can happen.

It was free choice time during class. Miss Fine, my student teacher, was busy in the room. Tara came up to me and asked, "Mrs. Harris, do you have a dick?" Of course I wondered why she was asking me this question. Out loud I asked her to repeat the question, thinking that perhaps the noise in the room had obscured her voice. She repeated the same question.

I took a quick inventory of what I knew about Tara. She had an older sister in second grade. She didn't seem to be that worldly that she would even know what a *dick* was. So, being the quick thinking and experienced teacher that I was, I refused the bait and instead asked her what that was. She was a bit perturbed with me for my ignorance, but explained it well, "You know, that thing you put in the computer. Miss Fine needs it."

Aha, a disc! Good thing I had asked, instead of getting all upset about the language this kindergartner was using and how rude she was. And I was grateful it wasn't a comment on my aging femininity. And, by the way, for any youngsters reading this...a disc was an item you inserted into the computer, long before a memory stick, or whatever is currently used.

*   *   *

On two occasions I was able to keep many of my kindergartners and take them with me to first grade. These were years that I cherished, as I could see so much growth in my students over the two years.

My now first grader, Lannie, came up to me one day with her writing book in hand. She showed me that she knew she had spelled the word "threw" correctly, although this was definitely not a word I expected her to know how to spell. She explained that last year, while in kindergarten, she would have spelled it "f-r-e-w" because that is how she pronounced it. Now that she was able to say it correctly, she could spell it the right way! We had a little celebration together.

I wonder why schools are asking youngsters to write with correct spelling, punctuation and capitalization so early, when some are still unable to produce the mature speech necessary to connect the printed word with what they are trying to say. It's my opinion that proper spelling does not correct immature speech.

*   *   *

Having time to observe students as they work and play is essential in getting to know more about them.

Observation is an essential part of being a teacher.

One day Noah asked me where the E was on the alphabet chart that had pictures. I told him it was with the elephant. He looked up, covered one eye to be able to find it, and then went about his writing. This seemed a bit unusual to me, so I mentioned it to his mom. I had only seen him do it this once. Mom took Noah to an eye specialist. It turned out that Noah had a cataract on his eye. At age five! Now he sees just fine.

*   *   *

Ernest was a shy boy and a gifted athlete who used to overlap images and letters in his writing and pictures. I called in the District Vision Specialist to observe him and she diagnosed him easily. As a result, his mom took him for vision training. Sometimes there are reasons for kids being shy, other than personality type. Perhaps they are protecting themselves due to an inability to perform tasks that we give them.

*   *   *

All teachers are asked to give standardized tests to their students. In kindergarten this included showing the printed letters and asking what sound each represented.

Lauren demonstrated her knowledge of letters and sounds one day without being given a test. She told me that someone in the class was using the *F* word. I asked her what the word was, but she told me she was not allowed to say it, so I told her she could whisper it to me and wouldn't get in trouble. Lauren came very close to my ear and whispered these two words, "Shut up."

There it was: a simple letter/sound recognition test on the spot! Lauren proved to me that she had not yet mastered the name of that letter and its sound. Or, perhaps that was her family's simplified version of what words were not acceptable in their household.

* * *

But that wasn't the only time I had to deal with forbidden words. I had adapted an old barbershop song for a song that my students and I sang each day as we were ready to leave the classroom: "Goodbye my class, well it's time to go," complete with us all singing the instrumental introduction, "Do, do, do, do, do" each time we sang that line. Towards the end of this short song, the words were, "I hate to leave you but I really must say," which was how we sang it for many years. Then Gina became my student.

After a few weeks of singing this song, she burst into tears during it. She explained that the word "hate" was a terrible word and she just couldn't sing it. She was correct. We changed the lyrics at the end to the more acceptable, "*I'd rather not leave you . . .*"

Point taken.

Chapter 5
RELIGION IN PUBLIC SCHOOLS

Let Us Pray! Let Us Not!

Religion in public schools? You might as well scream, "Fire!"

If you become a vocal music teacher and need to provide music for the December holidays I wish you strength. The important things to consider are not only the quality of songs, the appropriateness of arrangements for young voices and the variety of music, but they also must not include anything that smacks of religiosity. You must make sure the count of Chanukah and Christmas songs is obvious and equal. And even when the number is a match, it will not be obvious to everyone. You will receive at least one angry phone call from a parent who thinks that there has been unfair partiality.

December in kindergarten is a time when one needs to pay special attention to details. My students were rarely silent on the issues of religion, and they had very strong opinions. Their parents' opinions. In December, classroom conversations began something like this: "Are you Christmas or Chanukah?"

There was no evaluation or follow-up discussion. The children just seemed to be taking a survey. Sometimes I would hear a, "Me, too," but not much more than that.

Just as with the issue of equal time for holiday songs, the same accounting happened in a kindergarten class with the projects for the holidays. I believed in letting my students be free to create inventions of their own. Parents were quite used to their children bringing home boxes, tubes and all sorts of items taped and strung together. These were decorated with sequins, beads, markers, pebbles, shells, and any other sort of treasure each student could choose to express his artistic side. Children love to experiment with decorations, using items that they don't usually have at home but we provided at school. And their focus is on the medium, not the message. Many times Jewish parents received from their children a green and red Chanukah card decorated with a Christmas tree. Likewise, Christian parents often had their presents wrapped in paper colorfully decorated with blue *menorahs* and *dreidels*. I never heard any complaints about this.

After a discussion of the Christmas story, *The Polar Express*, I provided the children with ten inch, hard, cone-shaped items from a carpet store, inside of which I had taped a jingle bell dangling from a string, representing the bell that can be heard at the end of this magical Christmas story. The children decorated the outside of the heavy cardboard in any fashion that they chose.

Young Evan, prone to making up some wild stories, was in my kindergarten class that particular year. Evan's parents and I had laughed together over some of the tall tales he told. For example, he told me his dad was a doctor who flew his own airplane. Not true.

Evan's mom had been unsure whether to enroll him in public school or the local Catholic school. She had opted for public school, but wasn't fully convinced she had made the right decision. Her son's holiday art projects in our class did nothing to assure her. Apparently, she either missed my explanatory letter, or her son's decoration wasn't Christmassy enough. She was upset that while the students had made a Chanukah menorah on Xeroxed paper (something not very creative, but very recognizable), I had given them nothing to make for Christmas. I was concerned that she was so unhappy but I really had not short-changed her son's holiday, so I made sure that she understood our unusual Christmas project. Maybe she had never read *The Polar Express*, or perhaps she thought Evan's explanation was another wild one.

Eventually Evan's mom trusted me. The following year I took twenty of my thirty-three kindergarten students with me as I taught first grade. I made sure Evan's mom had the choice of me or another wonderful, first grade teacher who was Catholic. Evan remained my student for a second year.

I never got into discussions with my classes about religious practices, although I always encouraged students and parents to share their family customs with us. Over the years there were many wonderful displays, foods, songs and costumes that parents and their children lovingly brought to our classroom for all sorts of celebrations.

If you want to know what is *really* going on in kindergartners' minds, just remain a quiet presence while they are working and talking in a small group. Five-year-old philosophical discussions are quite entertaining. While they are busy cutting, tracing and gluing things together, some deep comments about God, death, and power will be discussed. I have had parent volunteers who were supervising such groups, report discussions both precocious and problematic. Some of these needed to be addressed by me, as per my principal's directive.

*   *   *

One comment came from Fran who said that, "the heathen Jews would not be going to heaven." Apparently, the volunteer parent supervising the group did not overhear this comment when it popped up around Christmas. But the remark made a big impression on my student, Kevin. He didn't mention it to his mom until several months later. Kevin was quite concerned. I don't remember if it was a general concern or if it was because he knew that I was Jewish. Kevin's mom had a heart to heart talk with him and helped put his mind at ease. Later, she brought the incident to my attention. It was the first I had heard about it.

I appreciated her telling me, and of her concern, not only for her son, but for Fran, who bore this news. Kevin's mom was especially helpful in class, and the manner in which she told me about this past event was with great care.

As an aside, Kevin's mom was especially keen on keeping her son germ-free. Every time she helped in the class, she noticed that when we gathered together and the students sat on the rug, Kevin would touch the soles of his shoes. This would throw her brain into overdrive. When we were finished on the rug she would take Kevin to the sink to wash his hands. I never noticed this. When she mentioned her sanitary standards for Kevin, I assured her they were not going to be met in her absence, and that I thought Kevin might just survive without all the soap and water. Fortunately she decided to go with my advice, and stopped the scrubbing, although she may have given him a complete delousing when he returned home each day. As I write this, Kevin is in medical school, no doubt already excelling at hand washing.

Okay, back to the issue of the heathens. I needed to have a conference with Fran's mom so I could inform her about the "heathen Jews" comment, even though it had occurred quite some time back, and then to help her plan how to talk with her daughter. Fran might have been concerned for my welfare as well as that of some of her classmates. Somehow Fran needed to understand that in our multi-cultural mix at school, it might be best not to share such sensitive information.

The conference went very well. Fran's mom was unhappy that her daughter had actually spoken those words, since they had never used that expression at home. I suggested that she might want to investigate the source before she spoke about it with Fran.

*   *   *

Another year, not around the holidays, a parent was supervising the students who were taking turns at the class computer. This was in the days when most children did not have computing devices in their homes. Larry was not pleased with another child having a turn first, so his reaction to not getting his way was to utter, "You Jew!" The child taking his turn was not Jewish and had no reaction to this outburst. The parent who was overseeing the computer, however, was Jewish and was horrified. She informed me right away. Not only did she inform me, she wanted to know how I was going to handle it!

Back to my principal for advice. My conference with Larry's mom was uncomfortable. My carefully thought out talk about this being a multi-cultural neighborhood and how it's important to respect everyone, really fell on deaf ears. Larry's mom just listened and when I told her what Larry had said, she didn't seem perturbed at all. She just said, "We don't talk that way." However, Larry never made the same mistake that I knew of. He was a very bright child.

Larry was not only bright, he also contributed a great deal in class. He had a lot to say. Larry noted with admiration how smart another boy in class was. At the same time he also volunteered the information to the class that he did not live in the school district. Days after this revelation, he raised his hand and said very earnestly, "Mrs. Harris, I cannot tell a lie! We don't live where we say we do!" I wonder how many times he had been told never to reveal this. Many times children hear only part of the sentence that begins with the word, "Don't." They hone in only on what follows "don't" and do the opposite of what we mean for them to do.

*　　　*　　　*

A Muslim family with a son in my class for two years, managed to avoid the December holiday frenzy altogether, by taking a family trip each year during this season. This was a good time for them to visit family members who lived far away. *I would have enjoyed a trip during this season myself!*

Because of Christian, Jewish, Islamic and even atheist sensitivities, I learned to avoid discussions of religious beliefs in class. It was too complex an issue for me to handle properly. Nevertheless, expect kindergartners to be really curious and open to talking about anything they have heard.

*　　　*　　　*

One unavoidable experience discussing religion in kindergarten had a happy ending but a precarious beginning that caught me off guard. It involved one of my most eager students – Xavier.

Xavier had never attended preschool and loved everything we did in kindergarten. Give him a piece of colored construction paper, crayons and scissors and he was in heaven. Form a circle and dance? Wowee! He was a teacher's happy dream of a student.

With thirty-three students working on a project at

tables, it was a rare moment in our class when the room was silent. Extremely rare. But this one afternoon was just such a day. I was walking around the tables, when Xavier raised and waved his hand excitedly. He scrunched up his face in a concerned manner and said, "Mrs. Harris, Mrs. Harris, did you hear?"

"Hear what, Xavier?"

"Jesus is dead!"

I could only guess that Xavier had just started religious school. You need to picture a really distraught, up-turned face of a child, waiting for some sage advice from me. I had just been walking around the room making sure not to trip over a chair or a stray foot sticking out, and *this* is the question I received? In my very best PC manner, I shook my head, pulled my lips in tight, hoped that my eyes appeared worried yet compassionate, and uttered the absolutely only brilliant words I could think of. "Yes, I've heard that."

At this point, Xavier threw down his crayon, gesticulated with both hands in the air and imploringly asked me, "What are we gonna do?"

Doing my very best, I called on all the wisdom I could muster and uttered these words, "I don't know."

Reader, do you remember the music for *The Lone Ranger* theme (The William Tell Overture)? Let the whole theme play loudly in your head. For right after my pathetic response to Xavier, without missing a beat, curly red-headed Monica, without even looking at us as we spoke next to her, saved the day. She kept on coloring and simply said, "Well, we've still got God!"

And with that, I could visualize someone in the room wipe his hands of the mess that was brilliantly handled by a five-year-old girl. Xavier appeared happier and Monica just kept on coloring. I nearly fell down with gratitude.

Imagine if adults could choose that power of simplicity and beauty in our complex world.

Chapter 6
THE WISDOM OF CHILDREN

Out of The Mouths of Babes

For my first year of teaching kindergarten, I learned by example, from the expert leader of our team of three, Sue Weaver. It was almost like being a student teacher again. Two of us were new to this grade, so we devised a plan to have our three classes arrive at staggered times, so that the two neophytes could watch how the lead teacher taught. We had three rooms to share together, one set up for free play time, another room for our centers' activities and tables, and the third for general gatherings with lots of room for making a circle for music, dance, drama, and talking together. The two of us got our kindergarten legs steadied and took off from there. Miss Weaver was masterful. She loved children, and most importantly, understood and appreciated children of this age. Her philosophy was infectious. We developed curriculum, shared ideas and helped in one another's classrooms.

After our first year together, we decided to get a pet

turtle for the classes. Feeling creative, our naming of the turtle proceeded in a quirky manner. We considered ideas such as Myrtle the turtle, Swifty, and Spot, but ultimately came up with the name Rabbit.

Naturally, our students laughed at this name, and it became a ready source of conversation and stories. As the year progressed the turtle's name was accepted like any other. It was no longer a topic of conversation, other than when Rabbit pooped. At least I thought it was not in the forefront of any of my thirty-three students' minds.

In those long-ago days of kindergarten, shortly after the school year began, each student received a home visit from his or her teacher. We would schedule a time during our planning portion of the day to go to each child's home as a way of bonding with our students, and to calm any fears about school. It was important to observe how our students acted at home, find out what they were interested in, and generally help them feel more comfortable about being in school.

I remember that my visit to Franklin's home lacked interaction. He had a brother who had been in kindergarten the year before, with one of my partner teachers. The brother was a verbal student, fluent in both English and his primary language, Chinese. However Franklin never spoke at school or when I visited him at his home. Franklin didn't interact with any of his classmates either. No laughter, no conflicts and no observable affects. He refused to participate in any activity, other than snacks and standing around at recess. I'm not sure if the current label "selective mute" had been invented back then, but Franklin might have qualified. However, a label doesn't change behavior. Appropriate intervention may help.

When I arrived at Franklin's house, I was greeted warmly by his grandmother. She became the spokesperson for Franklin. I would make eye contact with him and talk to him, and grandma would respond for him. After reading a book to Franklin we created our little beaded friendship pins, mine matching his, that we would wear the next day to school. It was a silent activity. We matched the next day but Franklin remained a silent observer at school.

During our Centers' Time I would make sure Franklin was seated at a table with other students. I offered him his materials and always gave him his choices of what he could do but he didn't respond. He only sat there, silent. Eventually I stopped giving him specific attention.

Two months into kindergarten Franklin had yet to participate in any manner, except for being ever watchful. He would allow me to read to him, but never made any comments about the books or pointed out anything I asked him to point to in a picture in the story. Franklin never showed any emotion, not even fear of being in kindergarten. He simply observed. I doubt that what ultimately happened would have been suggested by a therapist.

There was a portion of the day when the students had a long period of freely choosing from many activities. They could build with blocks, paint at the easels, read books, enjoy the playhouse, dress up clothes and other activities that brought them together in unstructured play. They learned how to share, solve problems and practice all sorts of un-testable skills. Rabbit, the turtle, was in this room for the children to play with.

Weeks after my visit to Franklin's house, he came up to me during this time of the day and stood quietly next to me. I said something to Franklin to acknowledge his presence. This day was different. This time Franklin looked at me and spoke. He said, very seriously and emphatically, "I have a pet rabbit and his name is *not* Turtle!"

This opened the floodgates of conversation and of speaking for Franklin. I responded by asking Franklin what the name of his pet rabbit was, and acknowledged with him that the turtle's name was very silly. He told me many things about his rabbit. I replied that I had not seen the rabbit on my home visit and asked more things about his pet. While we were talking I asked if Franklin would like to paint a picture of his rabbit. He wanted to, and we chatted more as I got the paper ready for him on the easel. While Franklin painted I stayed nearby. When he was finished, I asked if I could write what he wanted to tell me about his rabbit on his paper. He agreed.

I usually asked students to talk about their paintings for several reasons. First of all, their parents would be able to recognize what the artwork *was*. It was also another opportunity for the children to express themselves verbally. Franklin told me, in complete sentences, a great deal about his rabbit, without much prompting from me. From that day forward, Franklin became a fully participating kindergarten student! He talked with the other students. He picked up pencils and scissors, glue and crayons and began to create the way kindergartners do. He also played with the toys and ran and laughed with the other students outside. And, of course, he taught me something.

I think if we make things too perfect for children and leave out the chances for them to find problems to solve and make their own choices, we take away precious opportunities for them to learn. Given the time, the freedom to think divergently, the use of generic materials to create their own inventions, and the chance to work together with others, they can blossom.

Franklin certainly drove this lesson home to me. Perhaps a little bit of ridiculousness *can* bring out something magnificent!

While we are still on the subject of turtles . . .

*   *   *

Speaking with Nicole one morning, we started

discussing turtles. She liked them. I asked her if she had one for a pet, or had she seen them at the nearby lake. We talked about what turtles liked to do and what they ate.

I mentioned that when I was a young girl, my neighbors across the street had a pet turtle. One day they invited me to play with it in their backyard. While I played in the yard the lady of the house was gardening nearby and found a snail. She asked if I wanted to feed it to the turtle, and of course, I did. Snails were creatures that fascinated me, as long as I could wash away the slime and dirt after playing with them. The turtle ate the snail immediately. That was one less snail for my jar of salty water. When I found snails and brought them to the turtle, he obliged me by eating them all.

Let me digress again. In high school I had a most remarkable French teacher, Mr. Swan. I adored the language and I loved being in his classes. It so happened that he enjoyed eating escargots – snails. In fact, he would salivate profusely in class, talking about eating them with garlic butter. Mr. Swan had served in France in the Army during WWII, after which he lived there for a while. Our French class was fascinated by his stories. When I turned sixteen, my parents wanted me to choose a restaurant to eat at for my celebration dinner. I selected one where I could, for the first time, order escargots. My sister and my parents watched carefully when we were served. I was rather hesitant as I regarded my round plate, the indentations filled with turtle food. However, what's not to like about garlic and butter, even if what it covers is a bit chewy? No one in my family wanted a taste.

Back to my student, Nicole, and our discussion of snails. I confided in Nicole that I once ate snails that were served at a restaurant. I made a point of telling her they were special snails, not the ones found in our gardens.

Nicole watched me carefully, very carefully, with her big, expressive brown eyes. She was silent. I was beginning to get concerned that perhaps I should not have told her the story of my eating adventure, when she asked this telling question, "Were you a turtle when you ate the snails?"

Now it was my turn to have a long moment of silence. Nicole was capable of shifting between our adult reality and her imaginative, inner sense of the world. I asked her if she really thought I could be a turtle before I was a grownup. She paused a moment, probably knew what I hoped to hear, and then radiated a huge smile. She didn't answer me, so I'm not sure what she really believed. By chance I saw Nicole just before she entered college. She laughed when I told her of our kindergarten conversation. She didn't seem to have been harmed by it.

*   *   *

One of the many wonderful aspects of teaching young children is that they "buy in" to stories that most adults would consider just silly. Kids love silly. Many five-year-olds travel easily between reality and fantasy. Their ability to distinguish between real and pretend is not yet fully developed. What a joy it is, as a teacher, to participate in their sometimes magical views of life.

Children's literature takes advantage of this suspension of adult reality, especially in the wonderful illustrations in picture books. But then, isn't this also true for adults in the subjects of our movies, books, and games? Adults, supposedly, know the difference. However, the active imaginations of my students were not limited to books. They could easily be led to accept the idea that a friendly leprechaun or giant inhabited our classroom at night and would write and respond to their letters. Even my skeptical students eventually bought in to the presents he left them in the traps that they had concocted. My not-ready-for-prime-time writing students also found this a stimulating reason to write, draw, dictate and otherwise communicate by letter. If my students asked if something was really true, my response would frequently be, "What do you think?" This also led to some spirited conversations. Perhaps there was a part of me that wanted to revisit this special time in my own childhood.

*   *   *

One year my class was on a leprechaun hunt and, as we were returning to the classroom, the school custodian warned me to not let my students near a tall trash can that was next to our room. He had just trapped a rat and it was making a racket in the can. Can you imagine twenty five-year-olds *not* wanting to investigate anything that could possibly be a trapped leprechaun? I couldn't see us returning to the classroom until the rodent was gone, so we continued our search elsewhere.

*   *   *

When I was in elementary school we had a shade tree with a large sand box underneath. I spent many pleasurable hours there with my friends, tunneling in damp sand, until our fingers magically met as we completed a tunnel maze. Many years later, when a sand box was still allowed to exist on our playground, I was watering it down in the kindergarten yard, hoping it would become the right consistency for making tunnels the next day. Standing next to me were three boys, watching quietly. The boys were quiet. When Charlie asked what I was doing, I replied that I was watering the sand. They accepted this statement without comment. To be funny, I repeated my sentence with one little addition: "I'm watering the sand so it will grow."

The boys each replied with, "Oh." Just like that, they accepted what I said as true.

I began to feel a little guilty so I said, "You don't really believe that the sand will *grow*, do you?"

The boys, in turn, immediately answered, "No." They became quiet again and remained standing with me as I continued to water the sand. It was a pleasant activity in the afternoon heat. Even the sound of the water on the sand was soothing. A long minute later, Charlie announced that his father kept sand seeds in a bag in the garage.

This time I was the one to respond, "Oh."

Then Connor said that his dad had the same thing in his garage.

It became quiet again, after which Anthony declared, "You know that sand grows into rocks."

There was nothing more to be said.

From time to time events occur in our lives that don't make sense. Things we can talk about, laugh about, think about, weep about, and maybe even take action upon. Life is pretty mundane if there are not these pebbles or sometimes boulders that are placed in and around our paths. Finding a route over, around, or even including these rocks helps weave the tapestry of who we are. These rocks are the tests, the sparkling crystals that wait to be revealed. They are the toe-stubbers that create memories. They help us ponder, ask questions, and even solve problems.

Perhaps sand really *does* grow into rocks. Maybe a classroom pet with a silly name *can* promote thinking and change.

*   *   *

Occasionally I was privy to an "aha" moment in a child's school day. One such incident involved a former kindergartener of mine who was then in first grade. Louis came to me for help with reading and writing. He was writing something which required him to use the word "eye," but he was unsure about the correct spelling so he asked me. Since the goal of our work was to encourage him to write, I told him to jot down his guess and keep on writing. Louis wrote a capital I. When the writing portion of our work was done and we were reading a book together, just by chance, the book had the word "eye" in it. Louis zeroed in on this word, leaving the reading altogether, grabbed his writing paper and replaced the "I" with "eye." He was thrilled. This led to a talk about how difficult spelling with homonyms can be. For the rest of the year, when our paths would cross, we would quiz each other on this word. It was our fun little secret.

I like to cite this event as proof of what I had been taught. Reading really can make the important connection to writing, or spelling in this case. Spelling books that teach word families cannot address every child's best mode of learning. For some people drills and tests really help, but not everyone learns in such an organized manner. While I think these books have their place, spelling should be linked to reading, always.

*   *   *

Many years earlier, when I was a travelling music teacher at ten schools a week, my hours included time at a school where a classroom teacher was putting on the musical "Oliver." I had been scheduled to assist her. There were several older students who were cast as main characters in the show, but they were having great difficulty in learning their roles, because their reading skills held them back. The principal told them that if they couldn't do better at reading in general, in the classroom as well as their parts in the show, they couldn't have these desirable roles. These struggling readers were not easy to motivate, but here was a dangling carrot: if they improved their reading they could have the starring roles. And that's exactly what happened. Their grades improved, their behaviors changed, and they quickly became better readers. That principal knew his students very well! They gave their all, the musical was terrific, but most significantly, they became fluent readers. There were no physical bribes used in this case, just reality and consequences.

*   *   *

When my son was in first grade, he complained about a second grader who was always pestering him on the playground. I listened but I don't remember asking many details, because there were never any bruises involved. He said that no adult on the play yard had helped him when he complained. It turned out that I knew the *pesterer* from when I used to teach music at this school. I decided not to get involved in this problem, other than asking my son if he could avoid being around his nemesis. After a while, I got a note from the school, telling me that my son and this other child had been sent to the office for fighting on the playground. I wanted to know what had happened. According to my son he had taken just so much but couldn't take more and decided to handle the situation the only way he knew how. So he responded physically and the two of them were sent to the principal. That was the end of it. My son and I talked about his visit with the principal and what he learned. It wasn't a punishment that he received. Apparently, by being sent to the principal the problem was settled. He figured this, "if someone is being a total pest and won't stop, and no one else is helping you out with the problem, duke it out if you are the same size and are willing to risk a visit to the principal." And so he did and the pestering stopped.

Fast forward many years. Nick was my student with a similar problem on the kindergarten yard. Over and over he complained to me and to the aides on the yard. Nick was no shrinking violet. He was physically capable but had been taught to "use his words." I told him the story of my son, asked about Nick's persistent problem, and warned him that he might be risking a visit to the principal. But, if nothing else worked . . .

Apparently Nick discussed this solution with his parents. Before school started one morning I was in my classroom when the door *banged* open. I knew this was not the usual way for doors to be opened, but the emotional force of Nick's parents entering the room registered this way. His father, in particular, was adamant about discussing this problem and especially my suggestion to Nick. After all, they had made a big deal in their family about working things out verbally, and here I was, sabotaging their efforts. Dad reminded me that he was a lawyer and didn't think I should encourage his son to get in a fight. I agreed with him and explained just what had been happening to Nick, according to what I had been told. Our stories matched. I explained that, if Nick was willing to risk a visit to the principal, or some other such humiliation, that it just might do the trick. The parents relaxed, and thought about it. They didn't mention the word *lawsuit* which pleased me immensely.

I see Nick's mom at the grocery store now, from time to time. Nick has graduated from college, is doing well in the world, and we both chuckle at the kindergarten event. For the life of me, I can't remember if Nick actually tried it. Armed with the knowledge that he *could* do it, he may have caused a different sort of aura to exude from his mighty, five-year-old persona. I need to ask Nick's mom next time our paths cross.

*   *   *

With two whole years of music teaching under my belt, and realizing that I really didn't like traveling to ten schools a week, it was my good fortune that a unique principal welcomed me onto his campus as a 5th grade classroom teacher. I was unprepared, but excited at the prospect. I did lots of studying and researching over the summer, trying to imagine what it would be like. I absolutely loved it, and I adored my students. They were fascinating. The job was exhausting, but I was young and slept well. In order to continue as a general education teacher I started taking courses to complete a new teaching credential. To this day I remain grateful to my principal, Heber Meeks, who took on the risk of offering that opportunity.

One of my students that year had a very difficult time with reading. Sam was seemingly unable to read with any ease. I had had no training yet in teaching reading so I looked to experts for ideas. Vivid in my memory is a day that we were studying science. Sam found our study to be fascinating. He also found the same subject in an encyclopedia, written in language far beyond his ability to read. Sam asked to stay in at recess so he could read the article. And he read, aloud, and read and read. Was it finally a subject that he was passionate about that made him devour the pages? It was not easy for Sam to read, and he checked with me frequently, but he persisted and we were both extremely proud of his accomplishment.

Sam never made the leap from that article to reading in general in my class. But he certainly taught me an important lesson about the driving force of interest and focus. I was reminded of Sam, many years later, when I was tutoring Kevin, another 5th grader, who had absolutely no interest in anything "school-like." For months it was sloggingly difficult for us both. Until. . .

Kevin had a problem with the PE teacher at our elementary school. If his version of what happened was accurate then he had every reason to be upset. I don't remember the details, although Kevin probably does. He was beside himself with anger, humiliation, and tears. We talked about what he could do to communicate with both the principal and the physical education teacher. This became our first real writing lesson to have an important and immediate goal. Kevin wrote, we talked, he wrote some more, he wanted corrections, and he came up with a beautifully cogent letter that he was proud of. He turned it in at school and got positive results. Writing with a purpose made all the difference in Kevin's persistence.

* * *

On another occasion I had the privilege of witnessing the following miracle in my kindergarten class.

Nico was a rambunctious child in class. He had many underlying issues that I was then only just beginning to understand. Nico was in a chaotic and possibly violent family situation. He also had a lot to learn about being with other kids his own age. These tensions revealed themselves in a variety of inappropriate behaviors. Most of them were scary for his peers to deal with. Nico was basically a good kid whose impulses drove all that he did. It was no wonder that he was having difficulty making friends. I learned what helped calm him in class: water coloring, being read to and talking one on one.

At the suggestion of our school psychologist, I created a book for Nico with photographs and text. The photographs showed him interacting with his friends in the class. The text described the photos and emphasized that this is what friends do. We read it together and discussed it frequently.

Weeks went by, charts were made for good behavior and rewards were given by the whole class for Nico, but my arsenal of tricks was used up. I had had meetings with his parents, other teachers, the principal and the psychologist and listened to all their suggestions. I tried them all, unsuccessfully.

We gathered one morning on the rug, with its colored squares for seating. One quiet, very observant girl,

Olivia, patted the square next to her, right in front. She said, "Come and sit here, Nico, and be my friend."

Nico did. He just looked at her with adoration the whole ten minutes we were seated. He became calm in both body and voice. When we stood for the pledge, he stood and recited respectfully, hand over heart, eyes darting between the flag and Olivia. When we sang a patriotic song, he sang instead of shouting. He mimicked Olivia's every move. She just smiled and was the model student. Nico copied her exactly. And the day progressed magically.

The same scenario happened the following day. Only on this day, my other students had started to take notice. And they *really* wanted in on the action with Nico. He was a very charismatic person to be with. But Olivia somehow knew that her work was accomplished and she gracefully bowed out of the way, still his friend, but able to share him. The whole feeling of our class was transformed. In just two days Nico had learned how to be a friend and to accept the tentative, and then whole-hearted friendship of his classmates. It was so simple and beautiful.

I breathed a sigh of thanks every day after that, for my angel Olivia. I called her parents to share the story. They had no idea of what she had done, and had never said a word to her about what to do in a difficult situation like ours. They were thrilled · but not as thrilled as my whole class!

Unfortunately Nico's mother pulled him out of the class and enrolled him in another school for about two months. When he returned to our class my principal warned me that Nico could be coming back in a very angry state. In a chat with my students the day before he returned, we agreed that not all people are alike in personalities. We talked about how some classmates had become friends with Nico before he left, and they could still be friends now that he was coming back, even if he needed a little more help with friendship.

I decided to meet Nico before class began, while he was playing outside on the yard. When I came out, I found him easily - he was the blur, running around. Calling his name, I held out my arms. He squealed, ran over full force, and leaped onto me. Luckily there was a lunch bench nearby to sit on with him. Nico wasn't angry, but definitely back to his "beginning of the year" self. Olivia no longer intervened. At this point my students were older and more accustomed to his outbursts and power stances. They just weren't as fearful of him. As the year ended it was clear that some of his earlier progress had been lost.

I will never forget the miracle and wisdom of Olivia. It was a stunning lesson on the powers of love, acceptance, self-assurance, and of kindness, that were taught by one little five-year-old. Olivia was the youngest of four children whom I had the pleasure of teaching - all girls, all different personalities, but all absolutely lovely and loving, just like their parents.

*   *   *

Great Oaks from Little Acorns Grow is one of the English proverbs that I would use in my classroom. That's how I think of the story of Olivia and Nico. I used many of these sayings every year in kindergarten. Each day I would send two students to the office with the attendance and a proverb to recite to the office staff. "Stick together there's safety in numbers" was always the first one we recited each year. We discussed the meanings of some of them, once they were well-learned.

Ben and Will could barely contain themselves one Monday morning. They burst out with this big news: "We know what *many hands make light work* means! We went to a science birthday party and found out. We stood together in a line, holding hands while one person at the end of the line held a light bulb. On the other end of the line someone touched something and the light bulb went on!" Many hands make light work. Leave it to five-year-olds to figure out aphorisms.

Each day one of the students was our class' Special Helper. This person would take messages to the office, lead the pledge, choose a patriotic song for us to sing, set out the lunches and manage to care for other tasks that came up. One day I overheard Kevin explain this routine to a new student. "Mrs. Harris is very old and needs lots of help."

I wasn't sure if this was a new proverb or just stating the obvious. But that is five-year-old wisdom in a nutshell.

Chapter 7
TEACHING ADULTS

Learning at Any Age

For five years, while I taught kindergarten, I volunteered one evening each week to teach in an adult literacy program. Our community provided this valuable service and I was keen to be involved. At my school I was teaching beginning reading to children and was interested in how the process worked with adults who were learning or were struggling readers.

*　　　*　　　*

My first student was Terri, a woman who had never learned to read although she had graduated from high school. English was her primary language. She had been diagnosed as Learning Disabled in school, but didn't know why. Because of her reading deficiency Terri only frequented restaurants where there were pictures of the dishes to order. She had two daughters. Though Terri drove her own car I never asked her how she pulled that off. She somehow acquired a driver's license without being able to read. Terry's goal was to be able to write letters to her children's teachers, and to read the notes she received from them. She also knew that she could have a chance for a better paying job if she could read.

We met at the local adult school where I quickly learned that the materials they used did not appeal to me. Terri didn't like them either, so I brought in my own books and made up exercises for her. We worked together for three years. Early on in our meetings Terri asked how she would know when she became a reader. It was a question I had never been asked and I didn't have a good answer ready. We talked about how she was a smart person to be able to navigate in this world without reading. Riding home that night, I thought of an answer for her. I told Terri that she would know that she was a reader when she saw the signs in our environment and knew what they said without thinking about it. The next time we met I asked her what she thought about all the signs that bombard us. Terri told me she simply ignored them.

Have you ever thought about how difficult it would be to *not* read all the signs that give us information? Street signs, billboards, ads on TV, signs in the market, and freeway warnings are just a few things that Terri ignored.

Sometimes our sessions consisted of Terri dictating a letter to her daughter's teacher. Then our lesson revolved around the words and spelling, as she copied the letter over. She asked many questions about spelling.

Included in the materials I brought from home to help teach Terri were worksheets. She accepted these to work on, but she was very suspicious of the easy readers and children's books. I explained to her, more than once, that looking at pictures and the text together is an essential part of the reading process. Besides, many children's books have such talented illustrators, so it's a pleasure to read them, if only for the visuals. Eventually she got past the fact that she was learning from children's books and she realized that she could read these books to her girls - a new activity for them to enjoy together.

Toward the end of our three years together it was obvious that Terri was becoming a reader. She told me she no longer avoided looking at signs, but realized she was actually reading them. As a bonus Terri got a better paying job. She now only consulted with me about the letters she had written on her own, rather than waiting for me to take dictation that she would copy over.

Finally I was happy to bring in a book for her to read that was about a young girl's quest to teach her grandmother how to read. As she finished reading the book aloud, Terri saw the tears in my eyes. She didn't understand why I had become emotional. It was because I realized the ramifications of what she had accomplished, and how the book she had just read was really about her journey into literacy.

I have lost contact with Terri over the years and I wonder how her life changed as a result of our work together.

*   *   *

At the night school where we met each week, there were partitions between each tutoring work space. They did not reach the ceiling, so I could hear the voices of the people working around us. In particular, I became aware of how other tutors related and worked with their students. Mind you, this was all a purely volunteer endeavor, with each volunteer receiving just one training session. It was upsetting to me, however, when I overheard some of the negative ways the volunteers spoke with their students. Had I been a student, I'm not sure I would have returned for more harassing.

With my second student, I started writing my own little books, with more mature themes than those written for children, using a limited and controlled vocabulary. I even found clip art (these were pre-computer, internet days) to add to these books. Shane was living here in the United States, having grown up in Mexico. There he had attended school for just a couple of years, but hadn't even learned the alphabet, so we were really starting at the beginning. He also worked very hard to make ends meet and had no time, or perhaps no inclination, to practice on his own. Nevertheless he was a very personable young man. His vocabulary was fairly good and we got along well. We always returned to practicing the alphabet and letter sounds. I tried to teach him simple sight words so that he could read the very limited vocabulary texts that I created for him. These, along with some simple pictures and a humorous touch to the story line, worked well in establishing a few sight words for Shane.

After many months of meeting together, Shane stood up and held out his palms, separated from each other. He said, "I have the beans in this hand and the tortilla in the other one, but I haven't figured out how to put them together." That certainly summed up his difficulties, but I think he was also too distracted by his complicated life. He admitted that with his hard work schedule and a baby on the way, he never could spend any time to practice on his own.

*   *   *

I had to stop my volunteering after five years, as I was now deep into working on my Masters' Degree. This time *I* was the person who needed to make my already busy life less complicated!

Now that I am retired, still surrounded by all my children's books, I have a dream of using those books with adult learners in a classroom setting. Once I finish this book I hope to give it a try.

Chapter 8
FEARS

Nerves, Worries and Anxieties

We all experience fear. Sometimes it's justified – other times, unwarranted. But we all know this uncomfortable feeling and have had to deal with it. As adults we have a lot of experience with managing our feelings and responses. Children are just learning how to deal with fear and their responses are sometimes surprising.

I have a large collection of children's books that I used in my classrooms during my years of teaching. They were organized on my bookshelves at school so I could easily access the subjects I needed. I had a small collection in the Fears category. These had to do with death, nighttime noises, and physical ailments. These days bullying is a hot topic in education so I'm certain there are some good picture books that deal with this problem.

When faced with a troublesome peer, Bethany, a student in my class, just turned to him and declared that she didn't like how he was behaving, and that if he continued, she wouldn't be inviting him to her birthday party. He stopped annoying her.

But there were others who didn't have that self-confidence.

*   *   *

Children may hear something, and, while the event didn't actually happen to *them*, it makes a strong impression, so strong that it can sometimes translate in their young minds to having really happened to them - especially if it's something scary. The exact manner in which you question children is vitally important when fact finding.

Bailey, a gentle boy, was in my class with another student, Dorian, who was very controlling. I realized that Dorian was probably this way as a result of what was occurring in his home environment. I tried to be vigilant and keep him under control, but with thirty-three kindergartners in the class it was a constant concern. There is only a small difference between controlling and bullying. I would hold class meetings to address the issues, giving my students many opportunities to learn, watch, and act out scenarios that they could try when they felt uncomfortable or threatened.

Bailey chose to avoid playing with Dorian and I seated them apart from each other. However, they were near each other at snack time, or in impromptu groupings.

Bailey told his mother that Dorian had hurt him at school, but he didn't tell me. When Bailey's mom confronted me with this information it was news to me. I assured her that I was watching and listening as best I could, but since Bailey hadn't told me about it, I couldn't help him right after it happened. I encouraged her to talk with Bailey about how I could help if he would tell me at the time it happened.

This is not as easy as it sounds, especially for all five-year-olds. When Bailey reported yet another incident to his mom he again did not tell me. Mom told me and then decided to write a letter to the principal. Not remembering the event myself, I had a private chat with Bailey. As we spoke, it became apparent that Dorian hadn't actually done anything to Bailey. He simply had so much power in his verbal threats that Bailey thought the threat was carried out. The threat translated in his mind to have *actually* taken place. I spoke with my principal and she arranged to host a meeting between me and Dorian's parents. It sounded like a good plan, as my intervention had not been effective enough. We met, talked about Dorian's behavior in class and what could be done. The principal had brought Bailey's mom's letter to the meeting, as a reference. Unfortunately, the principal gently waved the envelope when she mentioned the numerous calls and letters she had received from other parents. It was a quick wave, but apparently slow enough for Dorian's mom to see and read the return address. Oops!

Need I tell you more? Dorian's mom called Bailey's mom, doing what Dorian did to Bailey, making threats. It was not pretty. Not only that, Dorian's mom didn't believe what we told her, so she came to class to observe. She got only a limited impression of her son's behaviors in class. Her remedy? Admonish him not to do something *after* he had just done it. She used a loud voice, too late to change things, and definitely not effective in stopping further similar behavior. Nothing was gained but additional noise in the classroom and no resultant change in Dorian. I knew that my suggesting more effective parenting techniques would have fallen on deaf and unwelcoming ears, so I didn't offer any.

At long last, one day Bailey came to me to report another of Dorian's transgressions. I was puzzled, as I had been right there when he said it occurred. Bailey kept his eyes averted while we talked, and was very quiet. He then admitted to me that Dorian hadn't *actually* done it, but that Bailey was very scared that he was going to hurt him in the future. There it was. He was scared enough to tell his teacher that it had actually happened, when it hadn't.

On another occasion, the reverse happened. A student *had* hurt his classmate, Nolan, even leaving a mark. Nolan told his parents that, despite his bruise, this particular child *never* hurt him and that he stayed away from this child, but that he hurt lots of other children. This was true for all the hurting that went on, but Nolan was in total denial of having been hurt, himself. The only way I knew that it had happened was that an aide on the playground told me about the incident. Nolan was a quiet child at school. Sharing a classroom with an unpredictable, troubled student, couldn't have made Nolan's school experience a positive one. When I made a home visit to Nolan I found that in fact, he was a very outgoing and happy boy away from school. I was glad to discover this but saddened to see what Nolan's school experience had become for him.

Each year that I taught young children, I gave my word that our classroom would be a safe place for them. In 2012, in spite of all my efforts and the efforts of the parents of my students that year, I could not keep this promise, and that's why it became my last year of teaching.

Chapter 9
FOUND TREASURES

Mining Gold in Kindergarten

If I would have taken video of some of the antics of my students through the years, I could have filled multiple memory sticks. Flashes of some of those moments bring me many private smiles.

I was on a home visit to Charlie, the oldest child in a family of three, soon-to-be four children. Charlie was settling in next to me on the couch so we could read a book together. Charlie's mom came over and quietly asked if her daughter could join us, and sit next to me. It was fine with me. As we made room for Bridget on the other side of me, her mom whispered that she would probably want to stroke my ear lobe while I read, and would I mind? I told her that would be just fine. And the three of us read the book together. It was my very first, and last, ear lobe-stroking-while-reading by a three-year-old.

Two years later, Bridget was in my kindergarten class. She and Lucy became friends. Lucy was a thumbsucker, but only when she listened to stories. At a certain point the two girls worked out how to sit next to each other on the rug for stories, arms intertwined, with the correct hand for sucking never interfering with the earlobe stroking by the other. It would have made a lovely photo. It certainly has stuck in my mind for years without the benefit of film. Remember film?

*   *   *

Many years later, as my students were filling their backpacks with papers, lunches, jackets and treasures of the day, Quinn, a five-year-old, approached me for help. As I peered into her backpack to help her organize the contents, I noticed a paper with printing on it. I asked her what it was, thinking it might have been a note I needed to see. Quinn took it out and said she had written it (with Dad's printing) to help her friend in our class who was sad. I asked if I could read it and she replied, "Yes."

I was stunned as I read it. It was a friendship poem from her heart · as genuine and thoughtful and so very kindergarten in nature as it could be. And, just like the author it was wise beyond years. I asked her if we could use it as our poem to memorize in the coming week. She agreed. I also asked her if I could try to make it into a song and again, the answer was positive.

Giving it some thought over the weekend, I realized I could not do her poem justice, so I shared it with my husband, Ron, a songwriter by profession. He changed no words, just repeated one line, and created a beautiful melody and harmony for it. I arranged for Quinn and her mom to arrive at school early so they could hear what he had done and Quinn could give her approval. Quinn and her mom loved the song and approved it immediately.

My husband had written the music out, with Quinn's name as lyricist and his as composer. Once Quinn approved the song, he made an accompaniment track to use while we sang. We learned it and then every kindergarten class learned it. At the end of the year concert for families, all the kindergarten voices were raised in singing this sweet, universal message.

This song has carried me through many difficult times since then. Maybe the words alone will touch you as well.

"The outside is not that important
But the inside is.
The outside is not that important
But the inside is.
Your soul is the most important thing
It helps you through
A-ding-a-ling-a-ling,
It also helps you have love for your friends... like you."

If you are an aspiring teacher, a current teacher, or just interested in education, I hope you have found some worthwhile reading in this memoir. Perhaps I have shed a new light on what is involved in teaching. Remember the words to this song when you have those *ding-a-ling-a-ling's* that always accompany life. Especially when you feel like saying. . .

"Tell me again, you want me to do *what?*"

Made in the USA
San Bernardino, CA
27 July 2018